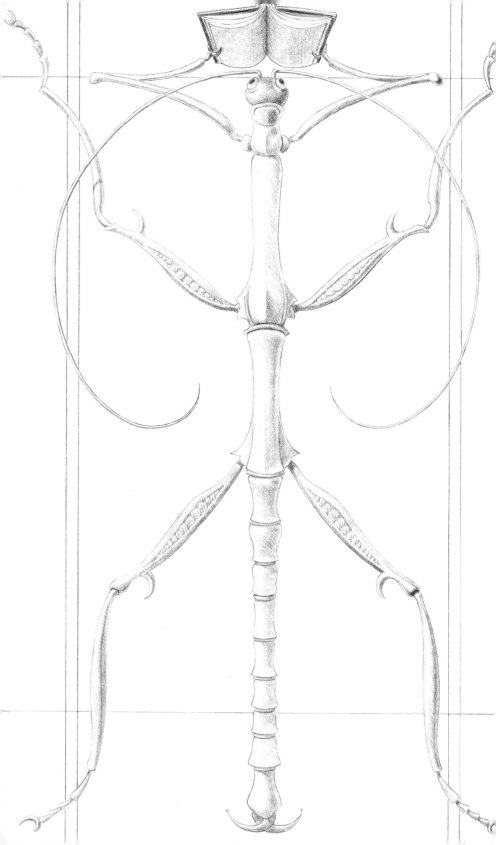

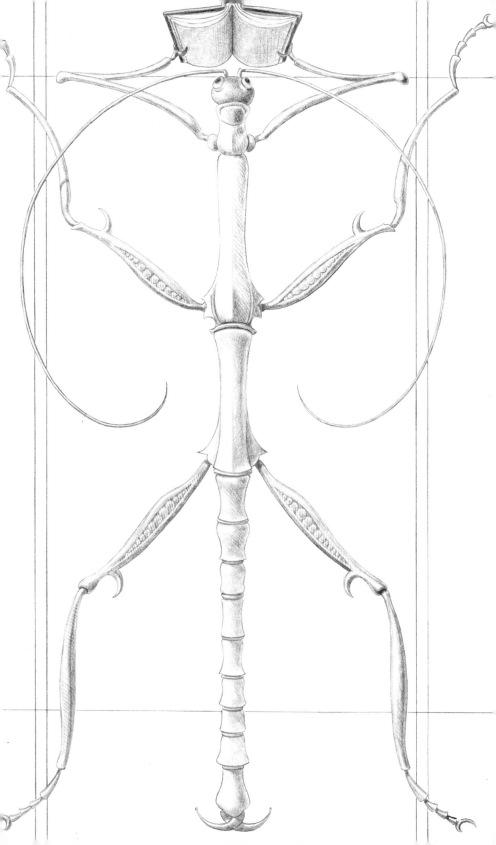

Also by Paul Fleischman

Poetry
Big Talk: Poems for Four Voices
Joyful Noise: Poems for Two Voices
I Am Phoenix: Poems for Two Voices

Picture Books
Sidewalk Circus
The Animal Hedge
Weslandia
Lost
Time Train

Novels
Breakout
Seek
Mind's Eye
Whirligig
Seedfolks
A Fate Totally Worse Than Death
Bull Run
The Borning Room
Saturnalia
The Half-a-Moon Inn

Nonfiction
Cannibal in the Mirror
Dateline: Troy

JOYFUL NOISE
Poems for Two Voices

JOYFUL NOISE
Poems for Two Voices

PAUL FLEISCHMAN
illustrated by Eric Beddows

A Charlotte Zolotow Book

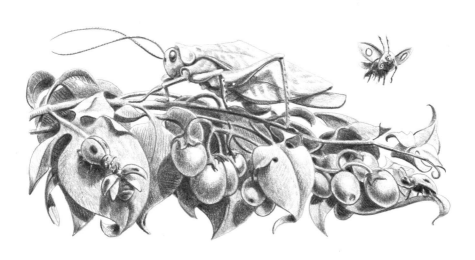

HarperTrophy®
An Imprint of HarperCollins *Publishers*

Library of Congress Cataloging-in-Publication Data
Fleischman, Paul.
  Joyful noise.
  "A Charlotte Zolotow Book."
  *Summary: A collection of poems describing the characteristics and
activities of a variety of insects.*
  ISBN 0-06-021852-5 — ISBN 0-06-021853-3 (lib. bdg.)
  ISBN 0-06-446093-2 (pbk.)
    *1. Insects—Juvenile poetry. 2. Children's poetry, American. [1.
Insects—Poetry. 2. American poetry.] I. Beddows, Eric, 1951– ill. II.
Title.*
PS3556.L42268J69 1988 811'.54   *87-45280*

Typography by Constance Fogler

For Seth, our porch light

P. F.

*for E. H. and Echo Hill Farm with its
wonderful fireflies*

E. B.

CONTENTS

NOTE

The following poems were written to be read aloud by
two readers at once, one taking the left-hand part, the other taking
the right-hand part. The poems should be read from top to bottom,
the two parts meshing as in a musical duet. When both readers
have lines at the same horizontal level, those lines
are to be spoken simultaneously.

JOYFUL NOISE
Poems for Two Voices

Grasshoppers

Sap's rising

Grasshoppers are
hatching out
Autumn-laid eggs

Young stepping

Ground's warming

Grasshoppers are
hatching out

splitting

into spring

Grasshoppers
hopping
high
Grassjumpers
jumping

Vaulting from
leaf to leaf
stem to stem
plant to plant

leapers
Grass-
bounders

springers
Grass-
soarers
Leapfrogging
longjumping
grasshoppers.

Grasshoppers
hopping

Grassjumpers
jumping
far

leaf to leaf
stem to stem
Grass-
leapers

bounders
Grass-
springers

soarers
Leapfrogging
longjumping
grasshoppers.

Water Striders

Whenever we're asked
if we walk upon water
we answer

To be sure.

Whenever we're asked
if we walk upon water
we answer
Of course.

It's quite true.

Whenever we're asked
if we walk on it often
we answer
Quite often.

All day through.
Should we be questioned
on whether it's easy
we answer

A snap.

Should we be told
that it's surely a miracle
we reply
Balderdash!

Nonsense!
Whenever we're asked
for instructions
we always say

and do as we do.

Whenever we're asked
if we walk on it often
we answer

Each day.

Should we be questioned
on whether it's easy
we answer
Quite easy.

It's a cinch.
Should we be told
that it's surely a miracle
we reply

Rubbish!

Whenever we're asked
for instructions
we always say
Come to the pond's edge

Put down one foot
and then put down another,

resting upon the thin film
on the surface.

Believe me, there's no call
at all to be nervous

as long as you're reasonably
mindful that you—

But by that time our student   But by that time our student
no matter how prudent
has usually

has usually
don't ask me why

sunk from view.   sunk from view.

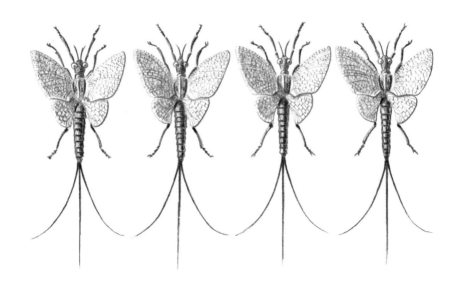

Mayflies

Your moment

        Mayfly month

Your hour

        Mayfly year

Your trifling day

        Our life

We're mayflies   We're mayflies

just emerging   just emerging

rising from the river,
born this day in May

    birthday

and dying day,

    this particle of time

this single sip of living

    all that we're allowed.

We're mayflies
by the millions
fevered

    We're mayflies
    by the millions

    frenzied

rushed

    no redwood's centuries
    to squander as we please.

We're mayflies
swarming, swerving,
rising high

    We're mayflies
    swarming, swerving,

    then falling,

courting on the wing,

    then mating in midair.

We're mayflies
laying eggs
our final, frantic act.

    We're mayflies
    laying eggs

light's weak

We're mayflies
lying dying
floating by the millions

from which we sprung
so very long ago

back when we were
young.

Sun's low

in haste we launch them
down the stream.
We're mayflies
lying dying

on the very stream

this morning
back when we were
young.

Fireflies

Light

Night
is our parchment

Light
is the ink we use

Night

We're
fireflies

(12)

fireflies
flitting

flickering

flashing

fireflies
glimmering

fireflies
gleaming

glowing

Insect calligraphers
practicing penmanship

Insect calligraphers

copying sentences

Six-legged scribblers
of vanishing messages,

Six-legged scribblers

fleeting graffiti

Fine artists in flight
adding dabs of light

Signing the June nights
as if they were paintings

flickering
fireflies
fireflies.

Fine artists in flight

bright brush strokes
Signing the June nights
as if they were paintings
We're
fireflies
flickering
fireflies.

Book Lice

I was born in a
fine old edition of Schiller

While I started life
in a private eye thriller

We're book lice
who dwell
in these dusty bookshelves.

We're book lice
who dwell
in these dusty bookshelves.

Later I lodged in
Scott's works—volume 50

While I passed my youth
in an Agatha Christie

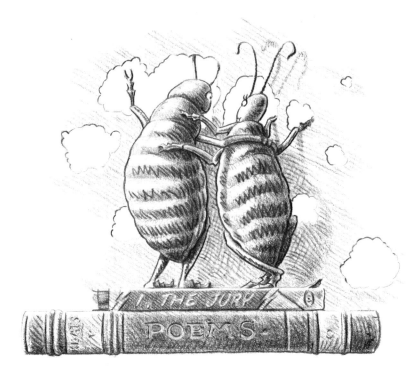

We're book lice
attached
despite contrasting pasts.
One day, while in search of
a new place to eat

We're book lice
who chew
on the bookbinding glue.
We honeymooned in an
old guide book on Greece

We're book lice
attached
despite contrasting pasts.

He fell down seven shelves,
where we happened to meet
We're book lice
who chew
on the bookbinding glue.

I missed Conan Doyle,
he pined for his Keats

We're book lice   We're book lice
fine mates   fine mates
despite different tastes.   despite different tastes.
So we set up our home
inside Roget's Thesaurus

Not far from my mysteries,
close to his Horace

We're book lice   We're book lice
adoring   adoring
despite her loud snoring. despite his loud snoring.
And there we've resided,
and there we'll remain,

He nearby his Shakespeare,
I near my Spillane

We're book-loving   We're book-loving
book lice   book lice
                    plain proof of the fact

which I'm certain I read
in a book some months back
that opposites   that opposites
often are known   often are known
to attract.   to attract.

The Moth's Serenade

Porch
light,
hear my plight!
I drink your light
like nectar

by day
Gaze in your eyes
all night
Porch light!

Porch
light,
hear my plight!

like nectar
Dream of you
by day

all night
Porch light!

I am
your seeking
circling
sighing
lovesick
knight
You are

my soul's
desire
my prize

Porch light!
My shining star!

"Keep back," they say
I can't!
"Don't touch," they say

Porch light!
Let's clasp
Let's kiss
Let's marry for a trice!

Bright paradise!
I am

seeking
circling
sighing

You are
my soul's
desire
my prize
my eyes'
delight
Porch light!

My compass needle's North!
"Keep back," they say

"Don't touch," they say
I must!
Porch light!
Let's kiss
Let's clasp
Let's marry for a trice!

Porch light!
Let's meet
Let's merge
Let's live for love!
For light!

Porch light!
Let's merge
Let's meet

For light!

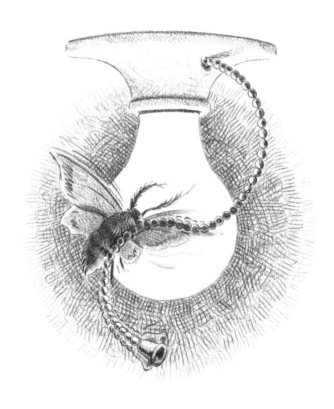

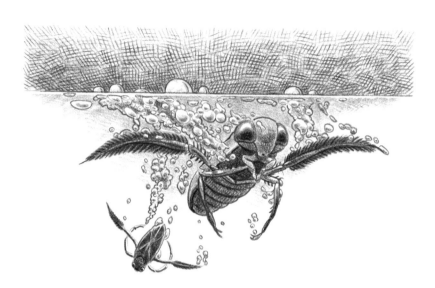

Water Boatmen

"Stroke!"
We're water boatmen
"Stroke!"

"Stroke!"
We're cockswain calling
"Stroke!"

"Stroke!"

"Stroke!"

"Stroke!"
up early, rowing
"Stroke!"

"Stroke!"
and oarsmen straining
"Stroke!"

and six-man racing shell
rolled into one.

"Stroke!"
worn-out from rowing
"Stroke!"

"Stroke!"
of this deep millpond
"Stroke!"

and shout the order
"Rest!"

We're water boatmen
"Stroke!"

"Stroke!"
Bound for the bottom
"Stroke!"

"Stroke!"
where we arrive

"Rest!"

The Digger Wasp

I will never
see my children,

they will never
gaze on me.

I'll have died

when they're emerging
next July.
So it must be.

So it must be.

I'm digging now
for their protection,

far underground,
they'll recognize
my deep affection.

stung and paralyzed,

for them to eat
they'll know as well
that I was wise.

in spite of every
interference,

and thieving beetles,
they'll discern
my perseverance.

Yet, when they
behold the home

safe and snug

they'll recognize
my deep affection.
When they hatch
and find a caterpillar,

left by me

they'll know as well
that I was wise.
When they learn
I'd dragged it there

weeds and rocks

they'll discern
my perseverance.
While, cocooned,

they pass the winter

safe from snow

and ice and chill,

they'll perceive

and thank me for

my formidable

my formidable

digging skill.

digging skill.

By the time they're

ready, next July,

to climb up from their cells

and break the burrow's seal

and fly away

my young will

my young will

know me well.

know me well.

When they care

for their own children,

never to be looked upon,

they'll feel my love

in replica

in replica

and know that they, in turn,

were cherished

by the mother digger wasp

whose face and form

whose face and form

they never saw.

they never saw.

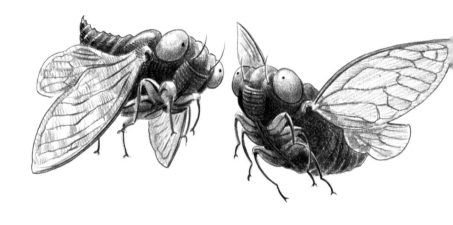

Cicadas

Afternoon, mid-August
Two cicadas singing

Five cicadas humming
Thunderheads northwestward
Twelve cicadas buzzing

the mighty choir's
assembling

Two cicadas singing
Air kiln-hot, lead-heavy
Five cicadas humming

Twelve cicadas buzzing
Up and down the street
the mighty choir's
assembling

Shrill cica-	
das	Ci-
droning	cadas
	droning
	in the elms
Three years	*Three years*
spent underground	
	among the roots
in darkness	in darkness
Now they're breaking ground	
	and climbing up
	the tree trunks
splitting skins	
and singing	and singing
	Jubilant
rejoicing	cicadas
	pouring out their
fervent praise	fervent praise
	for heat and light
their hymn	their hymn
sung to the sun	
Cicadas	Cicadas
	whining

whin-
ing

        ci-
        cadas
        whirring

whir-
ring

        ci-
        cadas
        pulsing

pulsing
chanting from the treetops   chanting from the treetops
sending
forth their   sending
booming   forth their
boisterous   booming
joyful noise!   joyful noise!

Honeybees

Being a bee

is a pain.

I'm a worker
I'll gladly explain.

I'm up at dawn, guarding
the hive's narrow entrance

Being a bee
is a joy.

I'm a queen

I'll gladly explain.
Upon rising, I'm fed
by my royal attendants,

I'm bathed

then I take out
the hive's morning trash

then I'm groomed.

then I put in an hour
making wax,
without two minutes' time
to sit still and relax.

The rest of my day
is quite simply set forth:

Then I might collect nectar
from the field
three miles north

I lay eggs,

or perhaps I'm on
larva detail

by the hundred.

feeding the grubs
in their cells,
wishing that *I* were still
helpless and pale.

I'm loved and I'm lauded,
I'm outranked by none.

Then I pack combs with
pollen—not my idea of fun.

When I've done
enough laying

Then, weary, I strive

I retire

to patch up any cracks
in the hive.

for the rest of the day.

Then I build some new cells,
slaving away at
enlarging this Hell,
dreading the sight
of another sunrise,
wondering why we don't
all unionize.

Truly, a bee's is the
worst
of all lives.

Truly, a bee's is the
best
of all lives.

Whirligig Beetles

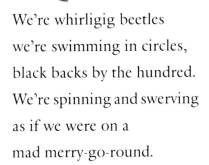

We're whirligig beetles
we're swimming in circles,
black backs by the hundred.

We're spinning and swerving
as if we were on a
mad merry-go-round.
We never get dizzy
from whirling and weaving
and wheeling and swirling.

We're whirligig beetles
we're swimming in circles,
black backs by the hundred.
We're spinning and swerving
as if we were on a
mad merry-go-round.

We never get dizzy
from whirling and weaving
and wheeling and swirling.
The same goes for turning,

The same goes for turning,
revolving and curving,
gyrating and twirling.
The crows fly directly,
but we prefer spirals,
arcs, ovals, and loops.

"As the whirligig swims"

circular
roundabout
backtracking
indirect
serpentine
tortuous
twisty,
best possible
route.

revolving and curving,
gyrating and twirling.

The crows fly directly,
but we prefer spirals,
arcs, ovals, and loops.
We're fond of the phrase
"As the whirligig swims"
meaning traveling by
the most circular
roundabout
backtracking
indirect
serpentine
tortuous
twisty and
turny,
best possible
route.

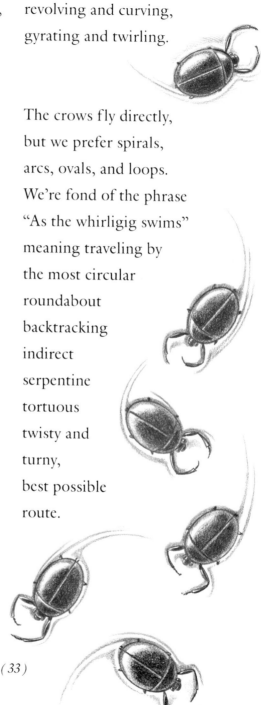

(33)

Requiem

Grant them rest eternal
Maple moths
Let light undying
shine upon them.

green darners
rest eternal

Carolina sphinx moths
Grant them rest eternal

Let light undying
shine upon them.
Praying mantises

rest eternal

Black-winged damselflies

brown darners
light undying.
Grasshoppers
great crested

three-banded
Katydids

northern

Cave crickets
mole crickets
tree crickets
field crickets

rest eternal

light undying.
This past night
we had the fall's first
killing frost.

light undying.
Grasshoppers

spur-throated

Katydids
round-headed

gladiator

Cave crickets
mole crickets
tree crickets
Grant them
rest eternal
Give them
light undying.

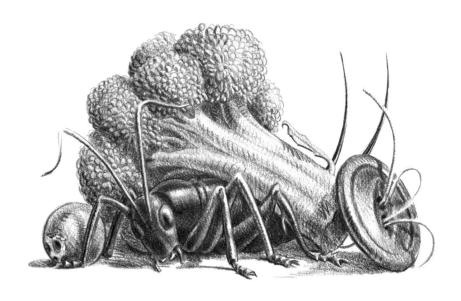

House Crickets

We don't live in meadows
crick-et
or in groves

crick-et
Others may worry

crick-et

We're house crickets
living beneath
this gas stove
crick-et

crick-et   crick-et
about fall

                        We're scarcely aware
                        of the seasons at all
crick-et   crick-et
Spring, to house crickets,
crick-et   crick-et
means no more

                        than the time
                        when fresh greens
                        once again grace the floor
crick-et   crick-et
Summer's the season
crick-et   crick-et
for pie crumbs:

                        peach, pear, boysenberry,
                        quince, apricot, plum
crick-et   crick-et
Pumpkin seeds tell us
crick-et   crick-et
fall's arrived

                        while hot chocolate spills
                        hint that it's
                        winter outside.

No matter the month
we stay well fed and warm,

For while others are ruled
by the sun in the heavens,

we live in a world
of fixed Fahrenheit
crick-et

our unchanging

steadfast and stable
bright blue
pilot light.

No matter the month

unconcerned about cold fronts
and wind chill and storms.
For while others are ruled

whose varying height brings
the seasons' procession,
we live in a world

crick-et
thanks to *our* sun:

reliable

bright blue
pilot light.

Chrysalis Diary

November 13:

Cold told me
to fasten my feet
to this branch,

to dangle upside down
from my perch,

to shed my skin,

to cease being a caterpillar
and I have obeyed.

and I have obeyed.

(*39*)

December 6:

                    Green,
the color of leaves and life,
has vanished!

                    has vanished!
                    The empire of leaves
lies in ruins!
                    lies in ruins!
I study the
brown new world around me.

                    I fear the future.

I hear few sounds.

                    Have any others of my kind
                    survived this cataclysm?

Swinging back and forth
in the wind,
I feel immeasurably alone.

                    January 4:
I can make out snow falling.

                    For five days and nights
                    it's been drifting down.

I find I never tire of
watching the flakes
in their multitudes
passing my window.

The world is now white.

Astounding.
I enter these
wondrous events
in my chronicle

Astounding.

knowing no reader
would believe me.

February 12:

An ice storm last night.

Unable to see out
at all this morning.

Yet I hear boughs cracking

and branches falling.

Hungry for sounds
in this silent world,
I cherish these,

miser them away
in my memory,
and wait for more.

ponder their import,

and wait for more.

March 28:

I wonder whether
I am the same being
who started this diary.

I've felt stormy inside

like the weather without.

My mouth is reshaping,

my legs are dissolving,

wings are growing

my body's not mine.
This morning,
a breeze from the south,
strangely fragrant,

my body's not mine.

a red-winged blackbird's
call in the distance,

a faint glimpse of green
in the branches.

And now I recall
that last night
I dreamt of flying.

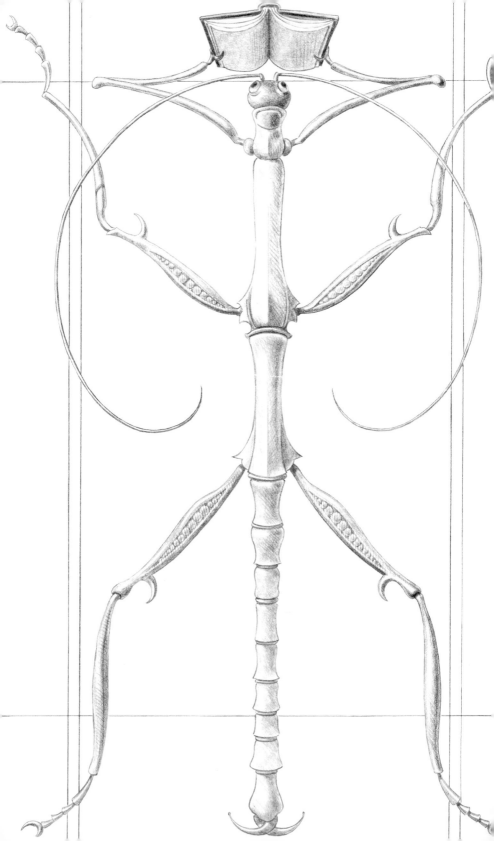

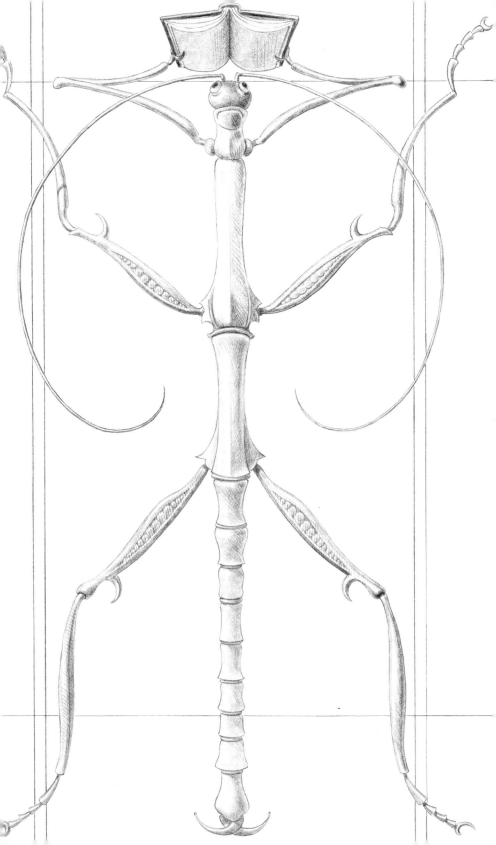